Wake Forest University has the best of two worlds — the good qualities of both the large university and the small liberal arts college. It is the skillful blending of these qualities and a fiercely guarded spirit of proud independence that give the university its particular mystique.

Sesquicentennial Commission, 1972

WAKE FOREST
UNIVERSITY

WAKE FOREST

A PHOTOGRAPHIC PORTRAIT

PHOTOGRAPHY BY KENNETH GARRETT

HARMONY HOUSE

PUBLISHERS LOUISVILLE

First Edition printed Fall, 1987
Executive Editors: Willam Butler and William Strode
Director of Photography: William Strode
Published by Harmony House Publishers, P.O.Box 90, Prospect,
Kentucky 40059
502-228-2010 / 228-4446
Printed in USA by Pinaire Lithographing Corp., Louisville, Kentucky
Hardcover International Standard Book Number 0-916509-17-6
Library of Congress Number 86-082739
Copyright © 1987 by Harmony House Publishers
Photographs copyright © Kenneth Garrett

Harmony House extends its grateful thanks to Dr. Edwin Wilson, Bob
Mills and Gareth Clement for all their help in the production of this
book. Thanks also to Dr. Margaret Smith, John Woodard, Bynum
Shaw, Dr. Thomas Olive, Dr. David Smiley, Judith Campbell, Cherin
Poovey, Alton Hill, and to the Offices of Sports Information and
Public Information.

Portrait of Dr. Samuel Wait, founder

11

OUR EYES SHALL SEE THE BEAUTY

By Dr. Edwin G. Wilson ('43)
Provost, Wake Forest University

A student from the treeless plains of the Midwest once told me he came to Wake Forest simply because he liked the name. He used to walk on the campus during the hour or two just before and just after sunset, and we would sometimes meet and talk. His favorite spot was on the path, now a sidewalk, about halfway between the Reynolda Hall parking lot and the Library, where, he said, you could see a little bit of almost everything that makes up the campus. Others might prefer the "quad"—or the Plaza, as we used to call it—because of the chapel columns and the Reynolda Hall stairs and the elm trees and the sense of being warmly and protectively sheltered on all four sides, but he liked the lower campus where you could see a long way beyond buildings, especially if you looked west toward the setting sun.

I have often tested my student friend's thesis, usually in the late afternoon on my way home from the office. Most recently, I stood at his favorite place on the Saturday evening of Commencement weekend. Before me, when I faced east, were the tables, now almost empty, where seniors and their parents had been enjoying a celebratory barbecue supper. When I faced west, I saw, past the encircling trees of the campus border, the rose-colored clouds of another majestically beautiful North Carolina sunset. All around me, in every direction, were the grass, the trees, the paths, the buildings that make up, in fact and in memory, the place that the name "Wake Forest" has, since 1956, brought to mind.

Reynolda Hall, I thought, is the place where, for most students, the Wake Forest adventure begins—over there, in the rooms beyond the second floor windows, where Bill Starling or Shirley Hamrick or another admissions officer greets, with smile, handshake, and words of welcome, the high school students who have come to take a look at Wake Forest. On the campus tour that follows, they see, as in a preview of a coming attraction, the world that may someday be theirs: Wake Forest students easily and naturally at home on a campus they know intimately, from the soccer fields along Polo Road to the tennis courts behind the "women's dormitories." One alumna told me she chose Wake Forest by sitting on a bench in front of the book store and watching the students go by. Some of them glanced her way and spoke; others remained preoccupied with their own thoughts, perhaps about a quiz or paper lying just ahead; one faculty member stopped and said a few friendly and encouraging words. She decided, in that moment, that Wake Forest was her school: an intuition not all that different from the expectation of the midwestern boy who simply liked the name.

On the old campus in the village of Wake Forest there was also a sidewalk I particularly liked—remembered distinctly now only by those of us who are past fifty. It was the way we took when we went from Wait Hall toward the Church, magnolias on every side. To our left, through the trees, was the "new" chapel; just ahead were the Alumni Building and Hunter Dormitory, evocative symbols of the College's humbler past. I first met Dr. Hubert McNeill Poteat on this sidewalk: the classicist-organist-orator who was one of old Wake Forest's authentically great men. As he approached me, I was increasingly scared. What should I say? I mumbled, my voice breaking, "Good morning, Dr. Poteat" (I yet dared not say "Dr. Hubert"); he looked at me, the freshman, and replied cordially. I had passed the supreme entrance test, and I belonged.

All faculty members have classrooms or laboratories that they find, more than other rooms, congenial to their temperament. Mine is Tribble Hall C216, its windows visible from the Reynolda Hall-to-the-library sidewalk. It is plain and austere. Nothing invites attention other than a wall map of Great Britain, blotched and worn and almost unreadable, which I think hung in the 'big" Alumni Building classroom where I took Shakespeare under Dr. Broadus Jones forty-five years ago; a lovingly detailed map of the Canterbury Pilgrimage prepared by my Chaucer-infatuated mentor, Edgar Folk; and a framed sketch of "Old Slick" Sledd, who was Dr. Folk's mentor and whose stand-up desk is still used by English teachers of today who know him only as a dim figure of long ago. Otherwise, the room is like any other classroom anywhere—except for the faces that crowd into my mind as I look at the empty chairs and remember who once sat over there by the window or who always took that back seat in the far corner. And the awareness of continuity, from Sledd to Folk to today's senior who may someday be the teacher behind the stand-up desk, fills me with a sense of longing but also brings quiet reassurance.

From almost any site on the campus, by day or night, I can see, in its distinctiveness, the steeple of Wait Chapel: a spire that reaches above the other buildings and that, from some distance, announces the presence of the University. The chapel has been a setting for great classical music (Arthur Rubinstein, Leontyne Price, the Philadelphia Orchestra) and for popular entertainers (Joan Baez, Billy Joel, Simon and Garfunkel), as well as for orientations, convocations and graduations. It has been a place for fun, with unexpected prankish intrusions into the solemnity of the hall. It has also been a reminder of Wake Forest's origins and her history. Here we have heard the claims of faith and conscience: Martin Luther King, in 1962, telling us that the salvation of the world lies in a love that passes understanding, and Elie Wiesel, in 1985, speaking of the necessity of witness because the alternative, silence, means complicity and consent.

Such reminders of love and witness are true to the language of Wake Forest's ancient religious heritage, first made evident to me and to my classmates in the courses taught by Allen Easley and Olin Binkley and in the sermons delivered every Sunday in the free campus church. No experience in worship on the old campus, I think, quite matched the week of services conducted in 1953 by Dr. Robert McCracken of the Riverside Church of New York City. Twice daily, he spoke to a voluntarily packed church, and when he left to go home, hundreds of students and faculty members followed him to the train station to sing and to say goodbye. He liked to hear one hymn in particular:

> There's a light upon the mountains,
> And the day is at the spring,
> When our eyes shall see the beauty
> And the glory of the King.

For me, that vision of a "light upon the mountains" has exemplified what it was that nineteenth-century North Carolina Baptists—mostly poor, mostly rural—saw when they gathered, across the state, in their churches and sang "Blest be the tie that binds" and dedicated themselves to the founding of Wake Forest.

Mrs. Edith Earnshaw, who worked beside her husband in the bursar's office in old Wait Hall, encouraged me, when I was a student, to go to graduate school and then come back to Wake Forest to teach. It would be the ideal life, she said, except for one thing: I would always be saying goodbye. This spring, as I shook hands with 647 graduating seniors, many of whom I had known and would miss, I realized anew what she meant. College is a place of goodbyes, and the student who sat on a book store bench and pictured Wake Forest as her own will one day see that bench from the Commencement platform and realize that she is surrendering it, now and forever, to some unknown successor.

Wake Forest, more than most colleges, has learned the full meaning of good-bye. We once said a long and irrevocable farewell to an entire campus, and for a while we were without home or "mother." But we found a new place, and far from being deprived or abandoned, we came to realize the good fortune of having two homes: one serene, pastoral and almost hidden, bathed in "celestial light" and remembered as youth is remembered; the other higher in altitude and in promise and yet, possessed, too, of its own bright radiance. The two homes are, indeed, our past and our future: we comprehend both in a single continuing vision, and the "light upon the mountains" still shines.

In the late summer and early autumn the rituals of the new year will begin again, and we will discover once more that, if at college we are always saying goodbye, we are also always saying hello. The football players will run out in their warm weather uniforms for practice, dreaming that the season might bring another Saturday victory like the one that came in 1946 over a heavily favored championship team from Tennessee or the one that Jay Venuto and James McDougald took from powerful Auburn in the year of the Tangerine Bowl. The residence hall advisers will assemble; behind Wingate Hall Ed Christman will gather his staff for the ride to Camp Hanes; freshmen and parents will arrive, hopeful and wondering; student leaders and administrators will rehearse their orientation speeches; and the Winston-Salem campus will become alive in the freshness of another year.

What will the newcomers find at Wake Forest? What students have always found, I hope: a university that honors, first of all, a fundamental commitment to the life of the mind and to moral and spiritual excellence; a place where reason, imagination and faith flourish; a place eternally and fearlessly in pursuit of the truth; a place which is open, hospitable, generous, loving and free; a place which men and women of good will everywhere might, if they knew it, be happy to call home.

Edwin G. Wilson

A WAKE FOREST CHRONOLOGY

1834 Wake Forest Manual Labor Institute opened on the Calvin Jones farm near Raleigh.

1836 Euzelian and Philomathesian literary societies founded, serving as campus-wide social and forensic organizations for 120 years.

1838 Wake Forest Institute rechartered as Wake Forest College.

1862 - 1866 Civil War closed College.

1888 Wake Forest vs. Carolina, first participation in intercollegiate athletics, and the first intercollegiate football game in North Carolina.

1894 Law School established.

1902 Two-year Medical School opened.

1941 Medical School expanded to four-year Bowman Gray School of Medicine, established in Winston-Salem, and related to North Carolina Baptist Hospital.

1942 Women enter Wake Forest.

1946 The Trustees and Baptist State Convention accepted proposal from Z. Smith Reynolds Foundation to relocate Wake Forest in Winston-Salem.

1948 School,of Business Administration established.

1951 President Harry S. Truman spoke at groundbreaking ceremonies on the new campus.

1956 Wake Forest moved to Winston-Salem.

1961 Graduate School of Arts and Sciences established.

1962 Wake Forest desegregated undergraduate student body.

1967 Wake Forest rechartered as Wake Forest University.

1969 Charles H. Babcock Graduate School of Management begun. Undergraduate courses in business assimilated into the undergraduate college curriculum.

1970 First student elected to the Board of Trustees.

1973 Groundbreaking ceremony held for the Fine Arts Complex, later named the James R. Scales Fine Arts Center.

1974 Casa Artom, the University's residential center on the Grand Canal in Venice, dedicated.

1975 Led by All-Americans Jay Haas and Curtis Strange, Wake Forest won its second consecutive NCAA team championship in golf. Under Coach Jesse Haddock, the Deacons repeated in 1986.

1976 National Science Foundation grant to Department of Biology precipitated controversy with the Baptist State Convention of North Carolina over control of the University; Eugene Worrell gave the University a house in London for use in overseas programs of study.

1978 The American Association of University Professors' highest honor, the Alexander Meiklejohn Award for Academic Freedom, given to the Wake Forest Trustees for their handling of recent controversies.

1979 Wake Forest and the Baptist State Convention established the Covenant relationship.

1980 Undergraduate School of Business and Accountancy established.

1984 Wake Forest celebrated its sesquicentennial as its twelfth president, Dr. Thomas K. Hearn, Jr., began his tenure; Wake Forest alumni won the coveted CASE/U.S. Steel Award for sustained performance in alumni giving among major private universities.

1986 Autonomy of Board of Trustees assured through a new fraternal relationship established between Wake Forest University and the Baptist State Convention; The Z. Smith Reynolds Library added its one millionth volume.

1987 RJR/Nabisco gave Wake Forest its 520,000 square foot World Headquarters Building, the largest unrestricted gift in the history of corporate philanthropy.

I think that Wake Forest, at its best, encourages intellectual playfulness, in the best sense of that word, without abandoning the principle that an educated person must be a responsible person.

Maria Merritt ('87), Rhodes Scholar, 1987

Anthropology Laboratory

Wake Forest is not a monument of mere brick or stone or mortar. It is, rather, a monument of faith in man and love of God. And every Wake Forest alumnus knows that in Forsyth County as in Wake, Wake Forest College will ever remain true to its founders who established an institution that would extend the light of life to mankind.

Senator Alton A. Lennon ('29), 1953

Scales Fine Arts Center

*I remember Wake Forest with great beauty.
I hold the institution very close and dearly
to my heart.*

A.R. Ammons ('49), poet

Wake Forest is the only institution for higher education that I know of which offers at once intellectual excitement and personal, almost familial, involvement. Being at Wake Forest is like studying and teaching in the privacy of my own home.

Maya Angelou (LHD '77), Reynolds Professor of American Studies

Freedom of the mind and spirit are very, very important to us, and to the whole world today. And I believe the history of Wake Forest College has some significant lessons for us in this regard. Wake Forest College has given 117 years of distinguished service to education and religion in this State. Over the years, this College has sent thousands of graduates out through the land to positions of leadership and trust.

President Harry Truman, at groundbreaking ceremonies, October 1951

Main Lounge, Reynolda Hall

Left, Reynolda Hall

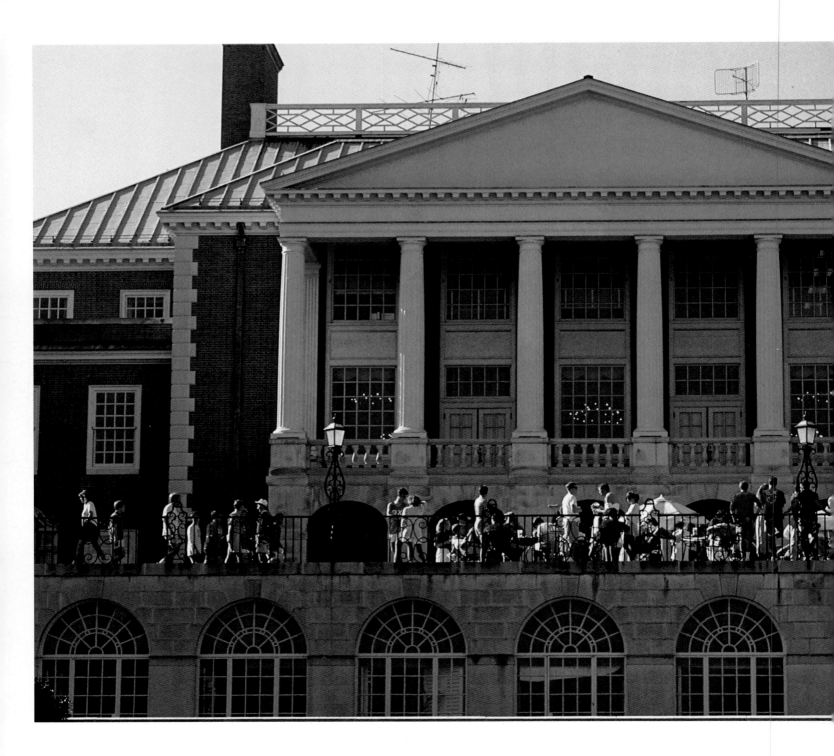

Wake Forest probably means a variety of things to different people, but there are some things which must be common to all the sons and daughters of Wake Forest. There is, for instance, the atmosphere of friendliness about the place.... there is absolutely nothing like it.

Bynum Shaw ('51), Professor of Journalism

Homecoming Class Parade

I find few who know where Wake Forest is, but I meet many who know where her sons are. The college is known by her fruits. She has spheres of influence in every field of endeavor, and her far-flung battle lines are holding their own. I voice their greetings and their grateful affection for Alma Mater.

James William Lynch (1888, D.D. '02), college chaplain ca. 1908

We give you here your place in the sun and beyond the sun.
We recognize your freedom in the noblest of liberties— in the
freedom of the soul.....We beg you realize your religion and
your life in your own experience; and whether you conform
to our view or not, we stand in reverence before you. We offer
you freely all we have; we impose nothing.

Senator Josiah W. Bailey (1893, LL.D. '31) Opening address, 1930

She is rowdy, but there are those who love her.

Gerald W. Johnson ('11, Litt.D.'28), author

I am proud of our institutional heritage. I believe in our sense of place and our sense of purpose. As we look to the future of Wake Forest, we shall not try to borrow our future from some other institution's past. We shall build upon the remarkable strengths and achievements of this institution. That is why and how our future shall arise from our past.

President Thomas K. Hearn, Jr.

University Theatre

Previous pages 52-53: The Dixie Classic Fair and Winston-Salem skyline; pages 54-55: Pilot Mountain

Watlington Hall, Bowman Gray School of Medicine

Electron Microscope

Bust of Charles H. Babcock,
Management School

Law School Moot Court Competition Awards

Law School Library

Scenes from the Graylyn Conference Center

Wake Forest has had a long and honorable career, and whether it nestles in a forest of Wake or stands on a knoll of Forsyth, its mission will remain a quest for truth and a crusade for simple right. We would not deny to this great institution and to those whose faith and good works have made it possible, this vista of a new dawn and this vision of a new hope.

Chief Justice Walter P. Stacy in *Reynolds Foundation, Inc.* v. *Trustees of Wake Forest College,* 1947

Provost Wilson and students on the Old Campus

Birthplace of Wake Forest, the Calvin Jones House

I wasn't the greatest student that ever went to Wake Forest, but I may have gotten the greatest education of anyone who went there. Wake Forest through the years to me was something that I could rely on. People would say, "Why are you still so active?" I don't think I could ever repay the debt I owe that university.

Arnold Palmer ('51, LL.D.'70), professional golfer

Golf Championship trophies

O, here's to Wake Forest,
A glass of the finest,
Red ruddy Rhenish filled up to the brim.
Her sons they are many,
Unrivaled by any,
With hearts o'er flowing we will sing a hymn.
Rah! Rah! Wake Forest Rah!
Old Alma Mater's sons we are,
We'll herald the story,
And die for her glory,
Old Gold and Black is ever waving high.

University Fight Song by C.P. Weaver ('04)

Have you forgotten the charm of the campus?
Shy, tender verdure when spring brought the robins;
Sweet shade in summer and scent of old boxwood;
Glory in autumn when maples were blazing;
Sunshine in winter on lustrous magnolias.
Have you forgotten, O son of Wake Forest?

Poem in *Alumni News*, March 1930

Path to Reynolda Gardens

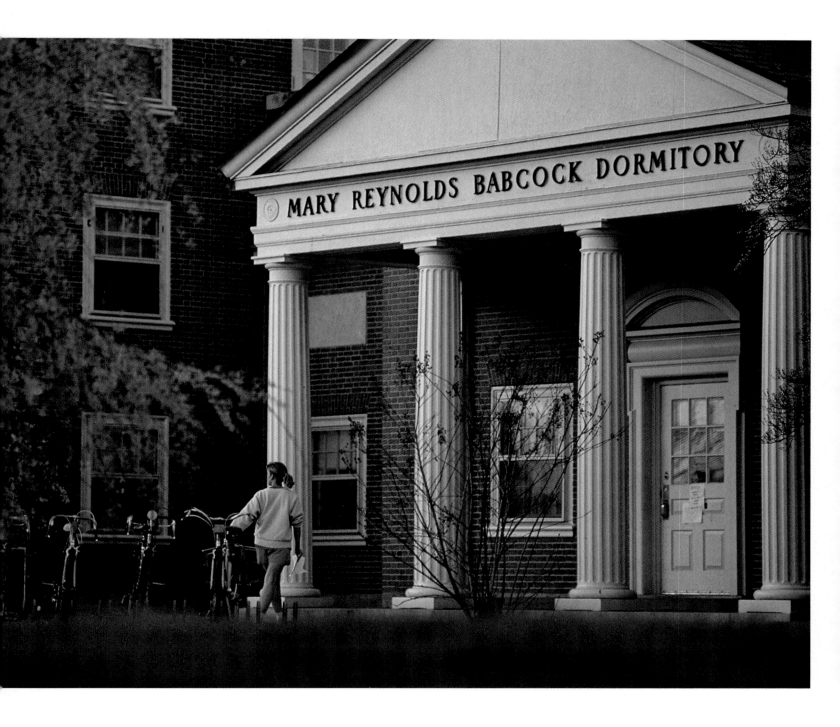

Moravian Love Feast, Wait Chapel

Z. Smith Reynolds Library

English Seminar Room

Brendle Recital Hall

We are not educating specialists for Broadway or Philharmonic Hall. We are educating the audiences and patrons who will keep alive those things which enlarge our sensitivity and raise our vision beyond the immediate and the vocational.

James Ralph Scales, President *Emeritus*

It is not meet for us to remain standing with our faces to the past, gazing at the fadeless tapestry into which is woven the spirit story of these hundred years. If we could see the invisible hands that wrought here, they would be pointing, not to the past, but to the future.

Thurman D. Kitchin ('05), University president, 1934 address

Art/Theatre Lobby

Scales Fine Arts Center

Few people, even the farsighted ones who brought Wake Forest to Winston-Salem, could have imagined the impact the University would have....It has enriched our lives.

Colin Stokes (LL.D. '77), Former Chairman, R.J. Reynolds Industries

RJR/Nabisco World Headquarters

Reynolda Gardens

Reynolda House

*When I hear that someone is denouncing my Alma Mater as a
nest of horrible antinomians, secular and religious, I am neither
shocked nor alarmed. I am merely satisfied that the old girl
remains true to the traditions that she cherished when I was
there; and as long as that is the case, I rest assured that the
State of North Carolina will never be wholly dominated by
politico-religious fanatics and cultural yahoos.*

Gerald W. Johnson ('11, Litt.D. '28), author

Rare Books Room, Z. Smith Reynolds Library

Baccalaureate service, Wait Chapel

Bowman Gray hooding ceremony

I think the most important lesson all of us learn at Wake Forest is not taught in any single classroom. Rather it's the result of our total experience here. And that lesson is a sense of community. A sense of ownership....We leave her with a commitment to the entire University family — the men and women around us, the alumni who preceded us, and the other students who will follow.

D. Wayne Calloway ('59), Chairman, Pepsico,Inc.

It is important for Wake Forest to have a particular sense of where it is. While the vision of any university is the world, home is North Carolina and Winston-Salem. We must maintain the record of service which this nstitution has given to the state and in recent years to this community. We are committed to the well-being of where we live. We want our presence here to be a positive, contributing factor to the life of the state and to the life of this community and more directly to our neighborhood.

President Thomas K. Hearn, Jr.

A BACKWARD GLANCE

A LOOK AT WAKE FOREST'S PAST THROUGH A SELECTION OF PHOTOGRAPHS FROM THE UNIVERSITY'S ARCHIVES AND COLLECTIONS

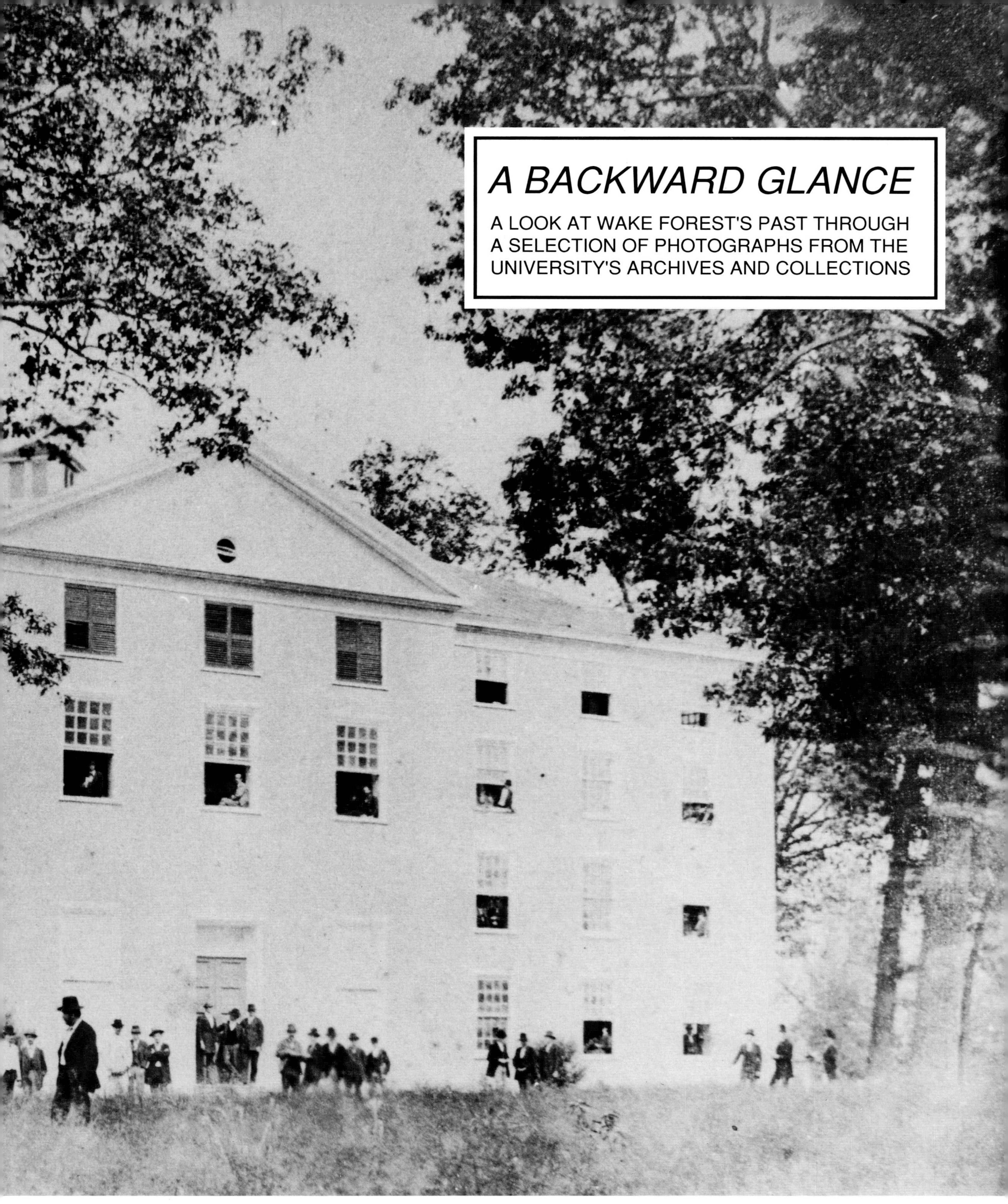

Perhaps the oldest photograph of the original Wake Forest campus, this picture shows the College Building, the first permanent building constructed on the campus. In this building were the chapel, classrooms, library and society halls, plus living quarters.

Dr. W.G. Simmons sits with six members of the Class of 1877:
(l. to r.) William Louis ("Billy") Poteat, E.E. Folk, J.R. Jones,
C.W. Scarborough, E.B. Jones and J.W. Denmark

The interior of the Library, ca. 1890.

This group, apparently the whole of the student body, gathered for a photograph in the spring of 1889.

Students pause for the camera in front of Wingate Memorial Hall, ca. 1888.

Arriving students and those who hopped the "Shoo Fly" into Raleigh came through this depot, shown here in 1909.

The front gates of Wake Forest College, prior to the arch, ca. 1900.

The Heck-Williams Library is shown here around 1888. This building, constructed in 1878, remained standing until 1956.

Wake Forest's first football team, 1888-1889. (l. to r.) White, Dowd, Williamson, Sikes, Merritt, Devin, Barnes, Richardson, McDaniels, Riddick, Oliver.

The football team, and goal post-standing fans, ca. 1890.

A baseball game in progress on the first athletic field, 1909

Academic procession, ca. 1906. Dr. William B. Royall and C.W. Scarborough, pastor, lead the procession.

The arch of 1909, a gift from the Class of 1909, is shown ca. 1911.

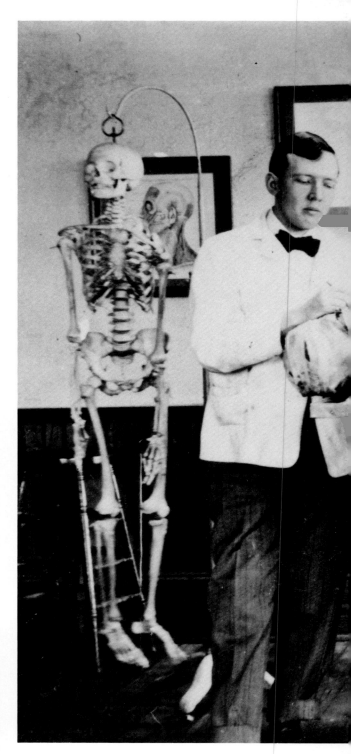

The arch approximately 20 years later, judging by the size of the trees.

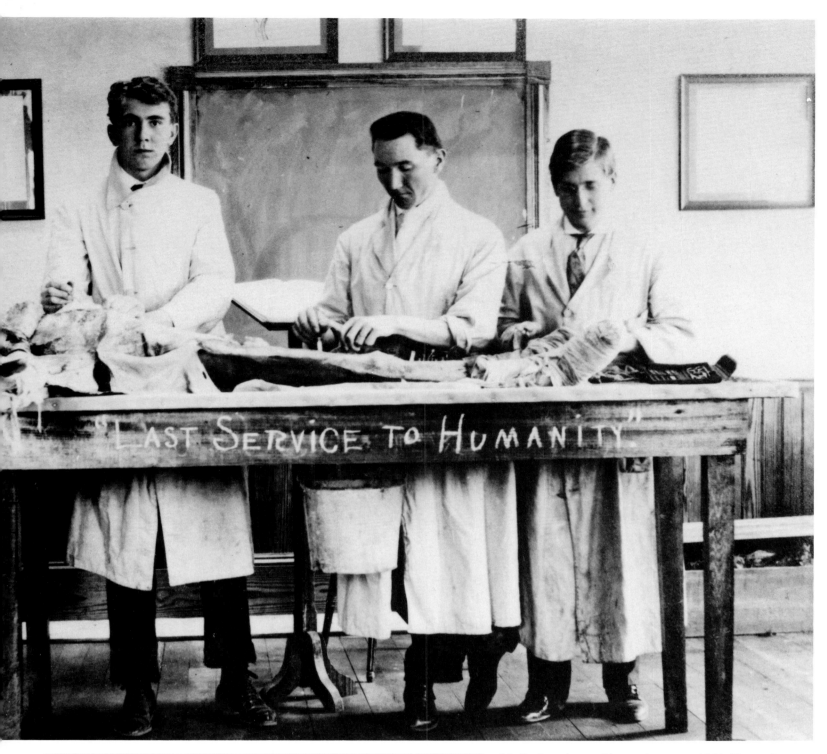

"LAST SERVICE TO HUMANITY"

Medical students with a cadaver, ca. 1910. The cadavers and skeleton were often used for pranks, usually against the "Frosh."

A typical student room at the turn of the century.

Panoramic view of the Wake Forest College campus, taken from the 1922 Howler.

Lea Laboratory, the fourth permanent building erected on the old campus, was used for both chemistry and biology classes.

A basketball game in progress in Gore Gymnasium during the 1930s.

Until the "Old Gymnasium," shown here ca. 1920, was built, students pursued athletics on the remodeled top floor of Wait Hall.

Bowman Gray School of Medicine and the North Carolina Baptist Hospital from the air in 1950. The medical school moved to Winston-Salem in 1942.

Wake Forest became coeducational in the 1940s.

Aerial view of the campus in 1940s, with Wake Forest Baptist Church in foreground.

Aerial view of the Reynolds Estate, the proposed campus location for Wake Forest, in the early 1950s.

The Wake Forest College Band spelling out "Peahead," the nickname of football coach Walker, at halftime of a game in the 1940s. The game is being played at Groves Stadium on the old campus.

The 1946 Deacon football team won the inaugural Gator Bowl game, defeating South Carolina 26-14.

Reynolda Campus, Winston-Salem, North Carolina, under construction in the 1950s. Buildings shown are Reynolda Hall, Davis Dormitory, and Z. Smith Reynolds Library in the background.

R.J. Reynolds, Jr. and Charles H. Babcock, both benefactors of Wake Forest University, flank architect J. Frederick Larsen as they look over plans of the Reynolda campus, 1956.